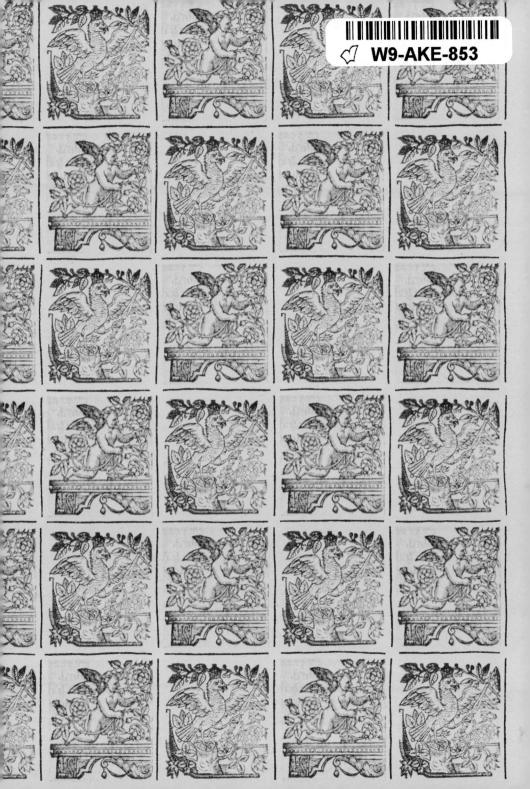

*for*

*Frederick*

*Ashton*

# ELIZABETH R

*Evocation*
*Roy Strong*

*Spectacle*
*Julia Trevelyan Oman*

SECKER & WARBURG · LONDON

First published in England 1971 by
Martin Secker & Warburg Limited
14 Carlisle Street, London W1V 6NN

SBN 436 50030 2


Printed in England by Westerham Press Limited, Westerham, Kent

Queen Elizabeth I's day began early. It started with the great curtains of her bed being drawn back by her Ladies of the Bed-chamber. The hangings were of cloth of silver trimmed with gold and silver lace and fringe. Together with the white satin ceiling to the tester they were painted with three hundred and forty-seven sprigs of flowers. The bed was of walnut, ornate with the Queen's Beasts in gilt and colour, while above nodded six huge bunches of multi-coloured ostrich plumes spangled with gold. Elizabeth had ordered this bed when she was fifty and it was designed to be taken apart for travelling, so that it could equally well have been at any of her palaces, Whitehall, Nonsuch, Greenwich, Windsor, Rich-mond, Hampton Court or Oatlands. The Queen's day, whether it was passed in one of these rambling Tudor palaces or in some nobleman's house, was always the same. Whatever the variants, it always began in the bedchamber. We know something of the appearance of Elizabeth's bedchambers. At Hampton Court there were rich coverlets of silk, at Windsor there was a table of red marble, a cushion worked by the Queen, a unicorn's horn together with a bird of paradise, while at Whitehall there stood by her bed a casket for jewels and 'other things of especial value'.

Elizabeth's day began among her women. These were the Ladies and Gentlewomen of the Bedchamber and of the Privy Chamber, headed by the Mistress of the Robes. Most of the Queen's closest friends had been one or other of these. Kate Ashley was her first Mistress, she who had been governess to Elizabeth at the age of four and had later sent Lord Admiral Seymour packing from the young Princess' bedroom. 'It was a shame,' she said, 'to see a man come so, bare-legged, to a maiden's chamber.' Kate Ashley was later succeeded by Lady Howard of Effingham whose death in 1587 'her Majestie tooke much more heavyly then my Lorde'. The keepership of the Queen's jewels was a separate office and entrusted to the capable hands of a formidable Welshwoman, Blanche Parry, who claimed to have rocked the baby Elizabeth in her cradle and whose epitaph proclaimed that she, like her mistress, had lived and died a virgin. Elizabeth passed most of her day with old friends and retainers such as these. To these we can add the Earl of Leicester's two sisters, Catherine, Lady Huntingdon and Mary, Lady Sidney, who had heroically nursed the Queen through smallpox, the Swedish Lady Northampton and, finally, Anne Russell, Countess of Warwick. Lady Warwick was 'more beloved and in greater favour with the . . . Queen than any other lady or woman'.

There were more troublesome additions, for serving the Queen also acted as a kind of finishing school and six young girls waited on her as Maids of Honour. The annals of the court are full of the travails connected with preserving the chastity of these all too often wayward nymphs. 'The queen hath of late,' observed Rowland Whyte, 'used the fair Mistress Brydges with words and blows of anger, and she and Mistress Russell were put out of the coffer chamber.' The fair Mistress Brydges had been too overtly the subject of the young Earl of Essex's attentions. Those ladies who married without her consent similarly received short shrift. Another gossip records that 'the Queen hath used Mary Shelton very ill for her marriage; she hath dealt both liberally in blows and words'. The main task of the Maids of Honour, however, was to act as a decorative foil to the Queen and to attend to her personal wants throughout the day. This included escorting her in the great procession to chapel each Sunday or waiting on her at table in the Privy Chamber. In the last years of the reign there seems to have been some unwritten rule that they always dressed in silver and white. Finally came lesser ladies who cared for quite menial tasks about the Queen, such as Mistress Bonne who looked after her ruffs.

Little is known of the details of Elizabeth's personal *toilette* on arising. She washed her hair with lye, a compound of wood-ash and water. One lye pot of the Queen's was of silver gilt and porcelain·with a comb case attached to it, another had a looking-glass. Once, early in the reign, thieves had broken into her lodging and made off with her lye pot together with other articles from her dressing table, her comb, a looking-glass and a gold bodkin used for braiding her hair. She cleaned her teeth by rubbing them

both inside and out with a tooth-cloth and using a toothpick. Beautiful gold-enamelled toothpicks were given her as presents by her ladies-in-waiting. Her teeth decayed badly as she grew older. One visitor records that they looked very yellow, another that they were black through consuming too much sugar. As many were missing it was difficult to hear what she said when she spoke quickly. In old age she relied heavily on cosmetics, mostly, probably, a lotion made of white of egg, powdered eggshell, alum, borax and poppy seeds mixed with mill-water. This strange liquid only blanched her skin, but by the turn of the century there are tart references to heavy painting, not only on her face but on her neck and bosom also. There is even a pathetic description of her cheeks being stuffed out with fine cloths to conceal the wrinkles and hollowness of her aged features. Many were the sweet smelling mouth-washes she could have used. 'Queen Elizabeth's Perfume' was made from marjoram. It was 'very sweet and good for the time' but fugitive, a contemporary wrote.

Francis Bacon records that 'she imagined that the people, who are much influenced by externals, would be diverted by the glitter of her jewels, from noticing the decay of her personal attractions'. No other English monarch had such an obsession with her own stage-management. Throughout her life the Queen led fashion and each day the decision about dress was important. Which of the hundred and twenty-five petticoats and sixty-seven round gowns would she wear? The vast repertory of hundreds of kirtles, safeguards, foreparts, mantles, veils, French gowns, round gowns and others, that made up her huge wardrobe must have made the combination of garments almost inexhaustible. As she advanced into the vale of years each public manifestation became yet more exotic. 'She was strangely attired in a dress of silver cloth,' reports a Frenchman in 1597, and she made a final spectacular appearance two months before her death to

receive the new Venetian ambassador, wearing hair, he reported, of a colour never made by nature.

The colours she liked best were black and white, which were especially 'her colours', worn by knights who fought in fancy dress in her honour or masquers who came to dance some complicated ballet. Much of her middle age was spent garbed in black with pearls looped across her bodice, a silver diaphanous veil encircling her, while in old age all was white and silver; even the Maids of Honour surrounding her were dressed in white, like bridesmaids, wherever she went. Both colours were flattering to the reddish-gold tinge of her hair and she carefully chose others to enhance it: russet and tawny, orange and marigold, peach and lady blush. Blue, green and yellow she practically never wore, except when they crept into the fringing and embroidery of her dresses and items of her accessories, fans and gloves, hats and muffs. Her passion for dress is reflected in the huge numbers of clothes presented to her as presents each New Year's Tide, from complete dresses to scarves and handkerchiefs. The task of dressing her must have been a long one on great public occasions when she wore elaborate gala attire as against the more simple dresses for everyday wear. The hands of her ladies must have grown tired as they worked pinning and tying into place layer after layer, working outwards from her smock to the minor details of attaching little jewelled pendants to the inside of some vast ruff or fixing a ribbon around her waist to carry a folding fan.

Over every garment ran a riot of embroidery depicting snails, worms, flies and spiders, rainbows, beasts and birds, flames, peascods and pillars,

*page 65*

My lord, Mr Shelton would have my Lady Elizabeth to dine
and sup every day at the board of estate. Alas, my lord, it is
not meet for a child of her age to keep such rule yet. I promise
you, my lord, I dare not take it upon me to keep her Grace in
health an' she keep that rule. For there she shall see divers
meats, and fruits, and wine, which it would be hard for me to
restrain her Grace from. Ye know, my lord, there is no place
of correction there; and she is too young yet to correct
greatly. I know well an' she be there, I shall neither bring her
up to the king's grace's honour, nor hers, nor to her health,
nor to my poor honesty. Wherefore, I show your lordship this
my desire, beseeching you, my lord, that my lady may have a
mess of meat at her own lodging, with a good dish or two that
is meet for her Grace to eat of; and the reversion of the mess
shall satisfy all her women, a gentleman usher, and a groom,
which be eleven persons on her side . . .

God knoweth my lady hath great pain with her great
teeth, and they come very slowly forth, which causeth me to
suffer her Grace to have her will more than I would. I trust to
God an' her teeth were well graft, to have her Grace after
another fashion than she is yet, so as I trust the king's grace
shall have great comfort in her Grace. For she is as toward a
child and as gentle of conditions, as ever I knew any in my
life. Jesu preserve her Grace!

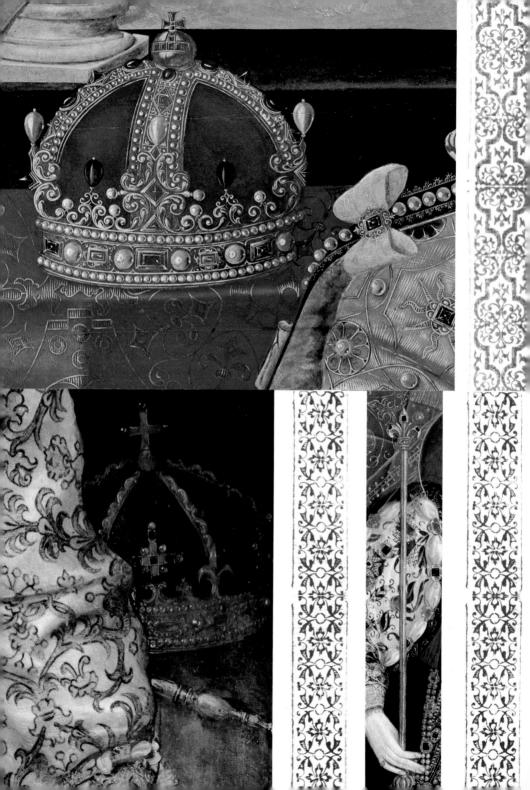

The ost followinge ij and iij in order     The Capytane of the ost     The m⁵ of the henchmen

*Here is my hand,*
*My dear lover England,*
*I am thine both with mind and heart,*

under the canapie borne by

The lord ambryse dudley leadinge the second fotter horse

The lord giles pawlet leadinge the firste fotter horse

The lord Robert dudley m⁵

 *For ever to endure,*
*Thou mayest be sure,*
*Until death us two do part.*

She took the cross-bow and killed six does and she did me the honour to give me a share of them.

Even by and by, her Majesty is going to the forest to kill some bucks with her bow, as she hath done in the park this morning.

From there we walked into the Queen's garden. In it there are thirty-four high, painted various animals of wood with gilt horns placed upon columns. On these columns are, further, banners with the Queen's coat-of-arms.

The hedges and surrounds were of hawthorn, bush firs, ivy, roses, juniper, holly, English or common elm, box and other shrubs, very gay and attractive.

There were all manner of shapes, men and women, half men and half horse, sirens, serving-maids with baskets, French lilies and delicate crenellations all round made from the dry twigs bound together and the aforesaid evergreen quick-set shrubs, or entirely of rosemary, all true to the life, and so cleverly and amusingly interwoven, mingled and grown together, trimmed and arranged picture-wise that their equal would be difficult to find.

And just as there is a park on the one hand, so opposite this in the middle of the other side there is a maze, similarly decorated with plants and flowering trees, and two marble fountains, so that time shall not drag in such a place; for should one miss one's way, not only are taste, vision and smell delighted, but the gladsome birdsongs and splashing fountains please the ear, indeed it is like an earthly paradise.

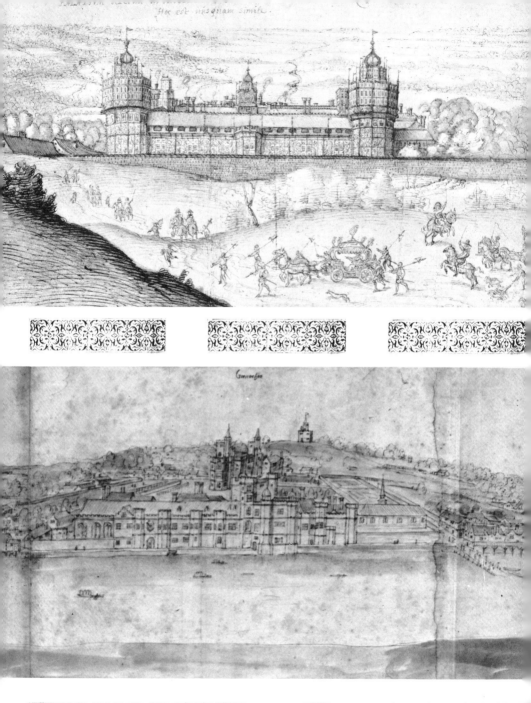

Hoc est magnam simile.

Greenwich

22

Lost from her Majesty's back the 17th of January, anno 10, R.Eliz. at Westminster, one aglet of gold enamelled blue, set upon a gown of purple velvet, the ground satin; the gown set all over with aglets of two sorts, the aglet which is lost being of the bigger sort. Mem., that the 18th of April, anno 8, R.Eliz. her Majesty wore a hat having a band of gold enamelled with knots, and set with twelve small rubies or garnets, at which time one of the said rubies was lost. Item, Lost from her Majesty's back at Willington, the 16th of July, one aglet of gold enamelled white. Item, One pearl and a tassel of gold being lost from her Majesty's back, off the French gown of black satin, the 15th day of July, at Greenwich.

Lost from her Majesty's back, the 14th of May, anno 21, one small acorn, and one oaken leaf of gold, at Westminster. Lost by her Majesty, in May, anno 23, two buttons of gold, like tortoises, with pearls in them, and one pearl more, lost, at the same time, from a tortoise. Lost, at Richmond, the 12th of February, from her Majesty's back, wearing the gown of purple cloth, of silver, one great diamond, out of a clasp of gold, given by the Earl of Leicester, parcel of the same gown 17, anno 25.

By the Earle of Northumberland, one jewell of golde like a lampe garnesshed with sparks of diamonds and one oppall.

By the Earl of Cumberland, a jewell of gold like a sacrifice.

By the Countesse of Bath, a fanne of swanne downe, with a maze of greene velvet, ymbrodered with seed pearles and a very small chayne of silver gilte, and in the middest a border on both sides of seed pearles, sparks of rubyes and emerods, and thereon a monster of gold, the head and breast mother-of-pearles; and a skarfe of white stitche cloth florished with Venis gold, silver, and carnacion silke.

By the Lord Seymer, a comfett box of mother-of-pearles, garnesshed with small sparks of rubies.

By the Barrones Lumley, a wastecoate of white taffety, imbrodered all over with a twist of flowers of Venis gold, silver, and some black silke.

By the Barrones Shandowes Knolls, a stoole of wood paynted, the seate covered with murry velvet, ymbrodered all over with pillers arched of Venis gold, silver, and silke.

By Sir Oratio Palavizino, one bodkyn of silver gilte, havinge a pendaunt jewell of gold, like a shipp, garnished with opaulls, sparks of diamonds, and three small pearles pendaunt.

By Mrs Blaunch Aparry, one long cushion of tawny cloth of gold, backed with taffety.

By Mr John Stanhop, a large bagg of white satten, ymbrodered all over with flowers, beasts, and burds, of Venis gold, silver, and silke.

By Mr Doctor Bayly, a pott of greene gynger, and a pott of the rynds of lemons.

By Mr Mountighu, one smock of fyne Holland and cloth, faire wroughte with black silke.

By John Smithson, Master Cooke, one faire marchpayne, with St George in the middest.

By John Dudley, Sargeante of the Pastry, one faire pye of quinces orringed.

The same day, after dinner, my Lord of Huntsdean drew me up to a quiet gallery, that I might hear some music (but he said he durst not avow it), where I might hear the Queen play upon the virginals. After I had hearkened a while, I took by the tapistry that hung before the door of the chamber, and, seeing her back was towards the door, I entered within the chamber, and stood a pretty space, hearing her play excellently well; but she left off immediately so soon as she turned her about, and came forward, seeming to strike me with her hand, alledging, she was not used to play before men, but when she was solitary to shun melancholy.

She takes great pleasure in dancing
and music. She told me that she
entertained at least sixty musicians; in
her youth she danced very well, and
composed measures and music, and
had played them herself and danced
them. She takes such pleasure in it that
when her Maids dance she follows the
cadence with her head, hand and foot.
She rebukes them if they do not dance
to her liking, and without doubt she is
a mistress of the art, having learnt in
the Italian manner to dance high.

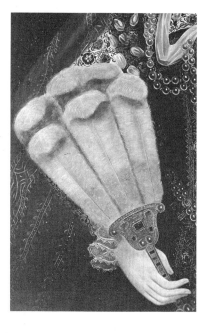

FANNES

Item, one fanne of white feathers, with a handle of golde, havinge two snakes wyndinge aboute it, garnished with a ball of diamondes in the ende, and a crowne on each side within a paire of winges garnished with diamondes, lackinge six diamondes.

Item, one fanne of feathers of divers colours, the handle of golde, with a bear and a ragged staffe on both sides, and a lookinge glasse on thone side.

FANNES

Item, one handle of golde enameled, set with small rubies and emerodes, lackinge nine stones, with a shipp under saile on thone side.

Item, one handle of christall, garnished with sylver guilte, with a worde within the handle.

Item, one handle of elitropia, garnished with golde, set with sparks of diamondes, rubies, and six small pearles, lackinge one diamonde.

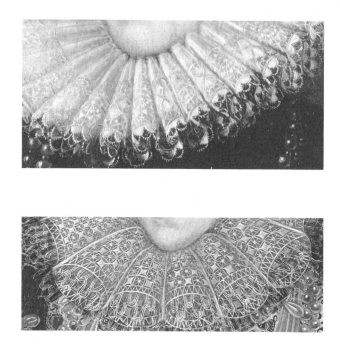

## FOREPARTES

Item, one fore parte of white satten, embrodered all over verie faire like seas, with dyvers devyses of rockes, shippes, and fishes, embrodered with Venice golde, sylver, and silke of sondrye colours, garnished with some seede pearle.

Item, one fore parte of white satten, embrodered all over with paunceis, little roses, knotts, and a border of mulberies, pillers, and pomegranets, of Venice golde, sylver, and sylke of sondrye colours.

Item, one fore parte of peach-colour, embrodered all over verie faire with dead trees, flowers, and a lyon in the myddest, garded with manye pearles of sondry sortes.

Item, one fore parte of greene satten, embroidered all over with sylver, like beastes, fowles, and fishes.

Item, one fore parte of lawne, embroidered with bees and sondrie wormes, lyned with white taphata.

### PETTICOATES

Item, one peticoate of watchet, or blew satten, embrodered all over with flowers and beasts, of Venice golde, silver, and silke, like a wilderness.

Item, one peticoate of white satten, embroidered all over slightlie with snakes of Venice golde, silver, and some owes, with a faire border, embroidered like seas, cloudes, and rainebowes.

Item, one peticoate of white Turquye satten, embrodered all over with a twiste of Venice golde, and owes like knotts.

Item, one peticoate of white satten, embroidered all over with Venice golde, silver, and silke of divers colours, with a verie faire border of pomegranetts, pyneapple trees, frutidge, and the nine Muses, in the same border.

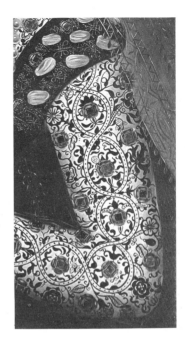

### FRENCH GOWNES

Item, one coveringe for a Frenche gowne of lawne, embroidered all over with fountaines, snaikes, swordes, and other devises, upon silver chamblet prented.

Item, one Frenche gowne of russet stiched cloth, richlie florished with golde and silver, lyned with orenge-colour taphata, and hanginge sleeves, lyned with white taphata, embroidered with antiques of golde and silke of sonderie colours, called china worke.

### ROUNDE GOWNES

Item, one rounde gowne of white cloth of silver, with workes of yellowe silke, like flies, wormes, and snailes.

Item, one rounde gowne, of the Irish fashion, of orenge tawney satten, cut and snipte, garded thicke overthwarte with aish-colour vellat, embroidered with Venice golde and spangles.

### CLOAKES

Item, one Dutche cloake of blacke vellat, embrodered all over with flowers and grashoppers, of Venice golde, silver, and silke, lyned with tawnie sarconet, furred with sables.

Item, one cloake of heare-colour raized mosseworke, embroidered like stubbes of dead trees, set with fourteen buttons embroidered like butterflies, with fower pearles and one emerode in a pece, lyned with cloth of sylver, prented.

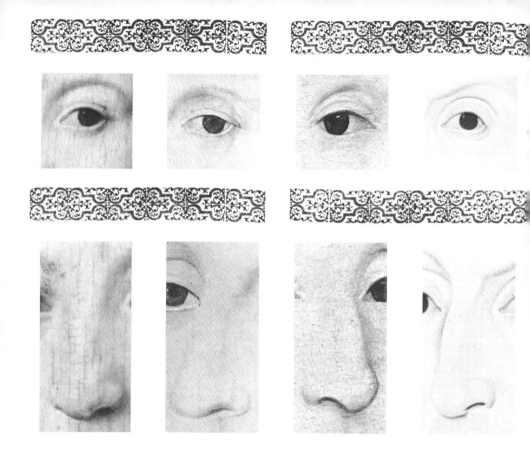

 When anyone speaks of her beauty she says that she never was beautiful, although she had that reputation thirty years ago. Nevertheless, she speaks of her beauty as often as she can.

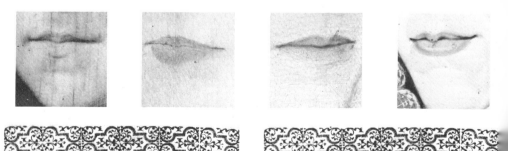

. . . she drew off her glove and showed me her hand, which is very long and more than mine by more than three broad fingers. It was formerly very beautiful, but it is now very thin, although the skin is still most fair.

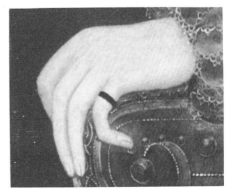

Next came the queen, in the sixty-sixth year of her age, as we were told, very majestic; her face, oblong, fair, but wrinkled; her eyes small, yet black and pleasant; her nose a little hooked; her lips narrow, and her teeth black . . . She had in her ears two pearls, with very rich drops; she wore false hair, and that red; upon her head she had a small crown . . . Her bosom was uncovered, as all the English ladies have it, till they marry; and she had on a necklace, of exceeding fine jewels; her hands were small, her fingers long, and her stature neither tall nor low . . .

Shee was a Lady, upon whom nature had bestowed, and well placed, many of her fayrest favores; of stature meane, slender, streight, and amiably composed; of such state in her carriage, as every motione of her seemed to beare majesty: her Haire was inclined to pale yellow, her foreheade large and faire, a seemeing sete for princely grace; her eyes lively and sweete, but short-sighted; her nose somewhat rising in the middest; the whole compasse of her countenance somewhat long, but yet of an admirable beauty, not so much in that which is tearmed the flower of youth, as in a most delightfull compositione of majesty and modesty in equall mixture.

He led me along a passage somewhat dark, into a chamber that they call the Privy Chamber, at the head of which was the Queen seated in a low chair, by herself, and withdrawn from all the Lords and Ladies that were present, they being in one place and she in another.

After I had made my reverence at the entry of the chamber, she rose and came five or six paces towards me, almost into the middle of the chamber. I kissed the fringe of her robe and she embraced me with both hands.

I did then live in the Strand, near St Clement's Church, when suddenly there was a report, (it was December, about five, and very dark,) that the queen was gone to council, and I was told, 'If you will see the queen, you must come quickly.' Then we all ran, when the court gates were set open . . . there we staid an hour and a half, and the yard was full, there being a great number of torches, when the queen came out in great state. Then we cried –

'God save your Majesty!'

And the queen turned to us, and said, 'God bless you all, my good people!'

Then we cried again, 'God save your Majesty!' And the queen said again to us, 'Ye may well have a greater prince, but ye shall never have a more loving prince.' And so the queen and the crowd there, looking upon one another awhile, her Majesty departed. This wrought such an impression upon us . . . that all the way long we did nothing but talk what an admirable queen she was and how we would adventure our lives in her service.

On the book: POSVI / TOREM / DEVM / MEVM / ADIV[...]

On the left medallion: HONI SOIT — QVI MAL Y PENSE

ELIZABETA D. G. ANGLIÆ, FRANCIÆ, HIBERNIÆ, ET VERGINIÆ
REGINA CHRISTIANAE FIDEI VNICVM PROPVGNACVLVM.

Immortalis honos Regum, cui non tulit ætas     Queis ipsæ tantum superant reliqua omnia regna,
Ulla prior, veniens nec feret ulla parem,     Quantum tu maior Regibus es reliquis,
Sospite quo nunquam terras habitare Britannas     Viue precor felix tanti in moderamine regni,
Desinet alma Quies, Iustitia atque Fides,     Dum tibi Rex Regum cælica regna paret.

In honorem serenissimæ Suæ Maiestatis hanc effigiem fieri curabat Ioannes Whitnelius belga. Anno 1596.

*My loving People, we have been perswaded by some that are careful of our Safety, to take heed how we commit our Self to armed Multitudes, for fear of Treachery; but I assure you, I do not desire to live to distrust my faithful and loving People. Let Tyrants fear, I have always so behaved my self, that under God, I have placed my chiefest Strength and Safeguard in the loyal Hearts and good Will of my Subjects, and therefore I am come amongst you, as you see, at that time, not for my Recreation and Disport, but being resolved, in the midst and heat of the Battle, to live or die amongst you all, to lay down for my God, and for my Kingdom, and for my People, my Honor, and my Blood, even in the Dust, I know I have the Body but of a week and feeble Woman, but I have the Heart and Stomach of a King, and of a King of England too, and think foul scorn that Parma or Spain, or any Prince of Europe should dare invade the Borders of my Realm; to which, rather than any Dishonor shall grow by me, I my self will take up Arms, I my self will be your General, Judge, and Rewarder of every one of your Vertues in the Field. I know, already for your Forwardness, you have deserved Rewards and Crowns; and we do assure you, in the Word of a Prince, they shall be duly paid you. In the mean time, my Lieutenant General shall be in my stead, than whom never Prince commanded more Noble or worthy Subject, not doubting but by your Obedience to my General, by your Concord in the Camp, and your Valor in the Field, we shall shortly have a famous Victory over those Enemies of my God, of my Kingdoms, and of my People.*

When I was fair and young and favour graced me,
Of many was I sought their mistress for to be,
But I did scorn them all and answered them therefore,
Go, go, go, seek some other where,
           Importune me no more.

How many weeping eyes I made to pine with woe,
How many sighing hearts I have no skill to show,
Yet I the prouder grew, and answered them therefore,
Go, go, go, seek some other where,
           Importune me no more.

Then spake fair Venus' son, that proud victorious boy,
And said, fine dame since that you have been so coy,
I will so pluck your plumes that you shall say no more,
Go, go, go, seek some other where,
           Importune me no more.

When he had spake these words such change grew in my breast,
That neither day nor night since that I could take any rest,
Then lo, I did repent of that I said before,
Go, go, go, seek some other where,
           Importune me no more.

The Latin, Spanish, French, and Italian she could speak very elegantly, and she was able to answer ambassadors on the sudden. Her manner of writing was somewhat obscure, and the style not vulgar, as being either learned by imitation of some author whom she delighted to read, or else affected for difference sake, that she might not write in such phrases as were commonly used. Of the Greek tongue also she was not altogether ignorant. She took pleasure in reading the best and wisest histories . . . For her recreations, she used them moderately and wisely without touch to her reputation or offense to her people. She was in her diet very temperate, as eating but of few kinds of meat and those not compounded. The wine she drank was mingled with water, containing three parts more in quantity than the wine itself. Precise hours of refection she observed not, as never eating but when her appetite required it. In matters of recreation, as singing, dancing and playing upon instruments, she was not ignorant nor excellent: a measure which in things indifferent best beseemeth a prince.

She was of nature somewhat hasty but quickly appeased; ready to show most kindness, where a little before she had been most sharp in reproving. Her greatest griefs of mind and body she either patiently endured or politely dissembled. I have heard it credibly reported that, not long before her death, she was divers times troubled with gout in her fingers whereof she would never complain, as seeming better pleased to be thought insensible of the pain than to acknowledge the disease. And she would often show herself abroad at public spectacles, even against her own liking, to no other end but that the people might the better perceive her ability of body and good disposition, which otherwise in respect of her years they might perhaps have doubted; so jealous was she to have her natural defects discovered for diminishing her reputation. As for flatterers, it is certain that she had many too near her, and was well contented to hear them.

FLOREAT · IN · ÆTERNVM ·

ROSA

ELECTA

HONI · SOIT · QVI · MAL · Y · PENSE

55

Her Highness hath done honour to my poor house by visiting me, and seemed much pleased at what we did to please her. My son made a fair Speech, to which she did give a most gracious reply. The women did dance before her, whilst cornets did salute from the gallery; and she did vouchsafe to eat two morsels of rich comfit cake, and drank a small cordial from a gold cup. She had a marvelous suit of velvet borne by four of her first women attendants in rich apparell; two Ushers did go before, and at going up stairs she called for a staff, and was much wearied in walking about the house, and said she wished to come another day. Six drums and six trumpets waited in the Court, and sounded at her approach and departure.

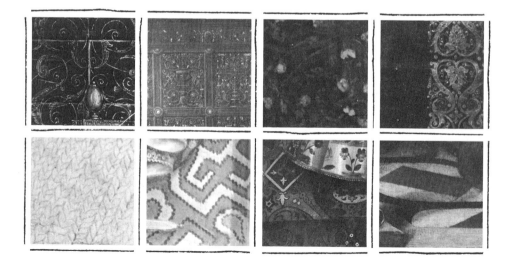

My wife did bear herself in wondrous good-liking, and was attired in a purple kirtle, fringed with gold; and myself in a rich band and collar of needlework . . . The Queen was much in commendation of our appearances, and smiled at the Ladies, who in their dances often came up to the stepp on which the seat was fixed to make their obeysance, and so fell back into order again . . . The day well nigh spent, the Queen went and tasted a small beverage that was set out in divers rooms where she might pass; and then in much order was attended to her Palace, the cornets and trumpets sounding through the streets.

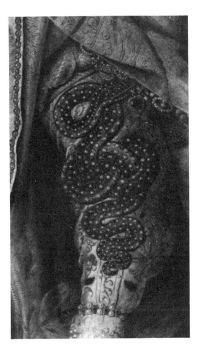

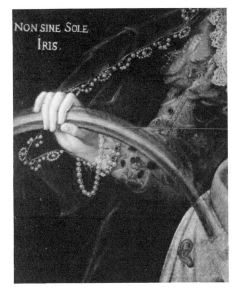

NON SINE SOLE
IRIS.

*Boy Jack,*

*I have made a clerk write fair my poor words for thine use, as it cannot be such striplings have entrance into parliament as yet. Ponder them in thy hours of leisure, and play with them, till they enter thine understanding; so shalt thou hereafter, perchance, find some good fruits thereof, when thy godmother is out of remembrance; and I do this because thy father was ready to serve and love us in trouble and thrall.*

*Mr Speaker,*

*... I do assure you that there is no prince that loveth his subjects better, or whose love can countervail our love; there is no jewel, be it of never so rich a price, which I prefer before this jewel; I mean your love, for I do more esteem it than any treasure or riches: for that we know how to prize; but love and thanks I count inestimably. And though God hath raised me high, yet this I count the glory of my crown: That I have reigned with your loves. This makes me that I do not so much rejoice that God hath made me to be a Queen, as to be a Queen over so thankful a people ...*

*I know the title of a King is a glorious title; but assure yourselves that the shining glory of princely authority hath not so dazzled the eyes of our understanding but that we will know and remember that we also are to yield an account of our actions before the great Judge.*

*To be a king and wear a crown is more glorious to them that see it than it is pleasure to them that bear it.*

*For myself, I was never so much enticed with the glorious name of a King, or royal authority of a Queen, as delighted that God hath made me this instrument to maintain His truth and glory, and to defend this kingdom (as I said) from peril, dishonour, tyranny and oppression.*

*There will never Queen sit in my seat with more zeal to my country, care to my subjects, and that will sooner with willingness yield and venture her life for your good and safety than myself. And though you have had and may have many princes more mighty and wise sitting in this seat, yet you never had or shall have any that will be more careful and loving ...*

*And so I commit you all to your best fortunes, and further counsels. And I pray you, Mr Comptroller, Mr Secretary, and you of my Council, that before these gentlemen depart into their countries, you bring them all to kiss my hand.*

62

*This morning about three at clocke hir Majestie departed this lyfe, mildly like a lambe, easily like a ripe apple from the tree . . .*

pomegranates, pansies and butterflies. The most dazzling attires must have been these embroidered ones, but the loveliest must have been those using transparent materials, tiffany, lawn or network. All that she wore was fragrant from storage with pretty embroidered sweetbags given her by her ladies each year, sachets full of lavender and other sweet-smelling preservatives. Each season and occasion called for its own particular form of dress. For the winter there were wonderful furs, lap mantles of plush or muffs of swansdown. For the great occasions of state, there were voluminous heavy robes of ermine and velvet to wear at the opening of Parliament or in the procession of the Knights of the Garter. Everything sparkled and caught the light when she moved, refracted from the hundreds of spangles, yards of gold braiding and myriads of little jewels on each dress.

Her passion for her clothes was matched by an equal fascination with jewellery. Late in the reign she was forcing the court on an exhausting progress to go where she had failed to reach the year before, bent on the journey because there were jewels and other presents which she had missed. Mary Queen of Scots' legendary black pearls came her way, as did the jewels of the impoverished Pretender to the Portuguese throne, Don Antonio. Her jewel inventory is a phantasmagoria running through carcanets, chains, 'flowers' or pendants, necklaces, rings, brooches, watches and bracelets. The jewels in their enamelled subject matter told a saga in themselves: suns, moons, flowers, fishes, gods and goddesses, all found their way onto the jewellery of Elizabeth I. In her dress and accessories the Queen was already a silent story to be read before the day had even begun.

After breakfast, which was of beef and ale, every morning began properly with the transaction of affairs of state with her secretaries and masters of requests. Letters were delivered to her kneeling, as indeed was all conversation conducted, until such time as she bade a man rise to his feet. No man ever wore a hat in the Queen's presence. Business was

undertaken in the Privy Chamber unless there was a formal meeting of the Council in the Council Chamber itself. Proclamations and all papers relating to public affairs had to be read and decisions given; huge piles of warrants had to be signed. We know that at Whitehall she had two little silver cabinets as writing boxes and her jeweller in 1589 gave her a small pair of writing tables of glass and silver gilt.

The architectural geography of Elizabeth's daily domestic life was always the same regardless of her residence. Wherever she went there had to be a bedchamber, a privy chamber, a presence chamber and a guardroom. More of her day was spent in the Privy Chamber than in any other room. Here she transacted most of her work, saw her councillors, ate her meals, read or made music, informally received ambassadors, entertained her friends, played cards and other games. Most palaces had other private rooms adjoining this. The Queen had an even more private withdrawing chamber, a privy gallery, privy garden and privy stairs by which to take to the river. These were her private domain, to which only those who were 'of the Privy Chamber' had admittance. Beyond the Privy Chamber lay the Presence, where the Queen ceremonially ate in public, through which the great procession to chapel passed, where ambassadors were received in state and where dancing took place. Anyone who could lay claim to being a gentleman had right of entrance to this room.

After the work of the morning the Queen often walked. Sir Thomas Smith parted from her at a Council meeting one December morning as 'she hasted to "go a-walking" with her ladies, because it was a frost'. Elizabeth was an inveterate walker to the end of her life. Even twelve months before her death the French ambassador records her taking her daily exercise of walking on Richmond Green. If the weather was intemperate she could stroll in the long gallery but most of all she liked the open air, even in the worst of weathers. As Leicester once wrote to Burghley, 'as oft as the weather serves, she hath not been within doors', and her last illness was brought on by a chill caught through having worn summery clothes when moving court one cold day early in 1603. The gardens in all the royal palaces were beautiful, gay with topiary hedges trimmed into exotic shapes, with shady green walks and plashing fountains. Their beauty was not only of greenery and blossom but above all of smell. Everything was scented and even the orchard was carpeted with sweet-smelling herbs. Elizabeth also loved flowers. Little posies were tucked into her bodice, a pink rose pinned to her ruff or spring flowers embroidered on her clothes. When she entertained foreign dignitaries, whole pavilions decorated with fresh flowers arose and even the floor of the royal barge was carpeted with fragrant blossoms. The Queen had a particularly strong aversion to bad smells. 'Tush man, your boots stink,' she had once remarked to some unfortunate courtier. Understandably she delighted in her godson Sir John Harington's discovery of the water closet which she installed at Richmond Palace, sending him thanks 'for his invention'.

Harington records too that 'Her Highness was wont to soothe her ruffled temper with reading every morning, when she had been stirred to passion at the council, or other matters had overthrown her gracious disposition'. In reading she had a particular taste for history and she sometimes diversified this by actually translating a classical author. Elizabeth had a brilliant, quick, natural intelligence and to spend part of the day translating lines of Boethius or Seneca would be entirely within the bounds of her character. She had been taught by a Renaissance man of letters, Roger Ascham, whose prize pupil she was. At sixteen she could speak Italian and French fluently and was well read in Latin and moderately so in Greek. Even in her sixties she was capable of springing up and delivering an oration in Latin or expressing herself when visiting one of the universities. Early in the reign she would read Greek and Latin with her old tutor; later his mantle fell onto the learned shoulders of Sir Henry Savile. Elizabeth also composed beautiful prayers in several languages, Italian, French, Latin and Greek. Indeed she took her religious duties seriously and was a woman whose devotion, less overt than that of her sister, was nonetheless a sustaining force in her life. In spite of all the contradictions of her character, there can be few royal deathbed scenes so exemplary as that of the great Queen as she crossed over the border of this life into the next assisted by her 'black husband', Archbishop Whitgift.

Food never particularly interested Elizabeth. She preserved to the end a thin wiry frame, healthy through vigorous exercise both on horseback and on foot. She never drank wine without mixing it with water and her dinner was always light, consumed in summertime in a room which overlooked gardens or some pleasant view, the windows being thrown open. Without, in the Presence Chamber, proceeded the ritual which she steadfastly avoided, the ceremonial eating in public. Often in summer, on progress, she ate in the open in the garden itself, her company forming a colourful group seated along a table laid in the cool of some arbour or walk. She always preferred to eat privately, alone or with very few people, and ate little. Even in the midst of the great fêtes at Kenilworth in 1575, the so-called Princely Pleasures, she 'ate smally or nothing'. She did, however, have a weakness for sweets. Gold and enamel comfit boxes were given her as presents and young Harington charmingly records that 'the Queenes Majestie tastede my wifes comfits and did muche praise her cunninge in the makinge'. The effect on the Queen's teeth of this penchant for sweet things has already been discussed. On the whole, however, Elizabeth, as a result of her diet and her passion for the open-air life, enjoyed remarkably good health. She had a deep aversion to being ill, preferring to suffer pain rather than admit that she had anything wrong with her. Her physicians once roundly told her that she had only been ill because of 'her contempt of physic and utter neglect of such potions as they considered necessary to keep her in health'.

After dinner, which lasted until about three, she sometimes used to rest but on other occasions it gave her pleasure to watch dancing in the Presence Chamber. This she did reclining on cushions, her ladies and favourites grouped around her, summoning young and old to come and talk to her. She always had a passion for the dance. At one period of her life she had danced five or six galliards every morning – even in her sixty-eighth year she was still capable of opening a ball with the Duc de Nevers – and she genuinely loved watching, beating time with her hands and correcting any dancers whose expertise she thought deficient. Elizabeth herself danced 'high' and because of this was known as the Florentine. It was quite usual for her to sit on cushions, spreading her skirts and trailing sleeves around her. The Queen liked sitting on the floor and cushions were warmly welcomed as New Year's gifts. In 1589 Mr Fynes gave her a long one of purple

satin embroidered all over with gold and seed pearls, trimmed with matching fringing and huge tassels.

During the summer months a large part of the day went on the chase in all its varying forms. At Cowdray in 1591, at eight in the morning she took horse and rode into the park where stood 'a delicate bowre' from which she shot deer with her crossbow. Later that day she watched sixteen bucks pulled down by greyhounds from the safe vantage point of a tower. But the chase could begin early in the morning and continue all day and include a picnic in the open. Travel on horseback, by water or coach also took much of the day. In the summer, when the court was on progress, several hundred carts meandered across the countryside while the Queen, seated in her coach, one of which was drawn by Pomeranian horses with tails and manes dyed orange, drove into the thickest part of the crowd to salute her people. Travel was not only tiring but difficult and distances covered were small. Generally the Queen made her next port of call early in the evening, about six, some time before supper. And nearly everywhere she went there was some form of entertainment to greet her. Sometimes it was listening to a lengthy oration by a dreary city orator, more often it was being met by characters from classical mythology or medieval romance. At Elvetham the court was welcomed by a poet and maidens who scattered flowers in the Queen's path. At Bisham, Lady Russell's two daughters played two virgin nymphs repelling the advances of a wanton Pan at the top of the hill down which the Queen rode to the house. And during the day such fêtes continued, from fairies dancing beneath her window in the morning to whole banquets being served in rooms made out of the branches of trees. Even when at home in her own palaces Elizabeth still enjoyed jaunts to see friends, although she did not like to return home empty-handed. 'The Lord Admiral's feasting the Queen had nothing extraordinary,' wrote John Chamberlain, 'neither were his presents so precious as was expected, being only a whole suit of apparel, whereas it was thought he would have bestowed his rich hangings of all the fights with the Spanish Armada.' Sometimes she helped herself. On visiting Lord Keeper Puckering at Kew 'she herself took from him a salt, a spoon, and a fork, of fair agate'.

In spite of her stinginess and sharp tongue, she was genuinely witty, loyal to old friends and very human. Time and again we catch glimpses of her humanity. She would stop her oration to the University of Oxford to see that Lord Burghley was given a stool to sit on to save his old legs or she would make a fuss of Lady Shrewsbury's little granddaughter, kissing her and pinning her dress properly into place. When she wrote a letter to a friend in distress, her usual tortuous style was abandoned in favour of one of startling directness. 'My own Crow,' she wrote to Lady Norris who had lost a son, 'harm not thyself for bootless help, but show a good example to comfort your dolorous yoke-fellow.' Lady Drury, 'my Besse', and Lady Carey, 'good Kate', similarly received moving letters of consolation from their 'most loving, careful sovereign'. Although she was personally averse to the idea of ill health, if it affected her friends she was entirely sympathetic and even fed Lord Burghley with her own hands during his last illness.

Supper, like dinner, was taken privately in the Privy Chamber where, in the evening, she relaxed with her friends and personal attendants, engaging in lively conversation, listening to music, playing cards or chess. 'They play at cards with the Queen,' someone wrote of Lord North and Sir Henry Lee. Sir John Stanhope, writing to Robert Cecil in 1598, gives a good account of the passing of an evening: 'Yesterday my Lord of Cumberlande was with her after supper; then my Lord H. Graye, and th' Erle of Rutland, with dyvers others, all nyght tyll 12 a clocke.' Elizabeth was extremely musical and music played a large part in any of her days, whether it was the splendours of John Bull at the organ in the Chapel Royal with the choristers singing the compositions of William Byrd, or John Hales, the celebrated lutanist, singing a song by John Dowland for the delectation of the Queen's company. She herself played both lute and virginals. She also sang and is recorded as having composed. Musical instruments are described as being in her private rooms and ambassadors frequently arrived to find her playing at her spinet. John Harington also wrote of his godmother that she 'loveth merry tales' and enough survives of her own repartee to capture the merriment that must often have surrounded her. She is a Queen who is frequently recorded as having been made to laugh. One anecdote ends with these words: 'Whereat her Majestie laughed as she had been tickled.' She had also the usual comic appurtenances of a Renaissance court: 'Jack Grene our foole', Thomasina the dwarf, 'William Shenton our Foole', 'Ipolyta the Tartarian' and 'a lytle Blackamore'. At certain times of the year the court in the evening would blaze forth in splendour, at Christmas and Shrovetide or on the reception of some great embassy. Then everyone would be in gala attire and there would be plays in the Great Hall or a masque performed in the Banqueting House.

The Queen's day ended where it had begun, in her bedchamber. Signalling to her guests that they should withdraw from the Privy Chamber, she retired, attended by her ladies. This time the toilette of the day was unravelled, the collage of jewels, lace, satin, velvet, veils, gold and silver was piece by piece laid aside and a few privileged eyes saw the Queen take to her bed in her nightdress of cambric wrought with black silk. When at last she placed herself between the sheets, 'worked all over with sundry fowls, beasts, and worms in silks of divers colours', and laid her head on her pillow 'of fyne cambricke, wrought all over with Venice gold and silke', yet one more day had passed in the life of that extraordinary woman, Elizabeth of England.

# Inventory of Spectacles and Evocations

**9**

THE YOUNG ELIZABETH

The face of Elizabeth I at about the age of fourteen

**10**

THE PRINCESS' GOVERNESS

Lady Bryan to Thomas Cromwell, 1536

*Lady Bryan, whose husband, Sir Thomas, was a kinsman of Elizabeth's mother, was entrusted with the office of governess. During the period following Anne Boleyn's execution the Princess was sorely neglected and Lady Bryan's letters tell of the travails of the young child who had 'neither gown, nor kirtle, nor petticoat, nor no manner of linen'.*

**11**

THE PRINCESS ELIZABETH

Elizabeth at about the age of thirteen

**12**

ACCESSION: CROWNS AND SCEPTRES

*Elizabeth was at Hatfield when her sister Mary died on November 17th 1558. On hearing the news she sank to her knees and repeated Psalm 108 : 'It is the Lord's doing, it is marvellous in our eyes.'*

**13**

THE CORONATION .

Queen Elizabeth I in her coronation robes

*Elizabeth made her state entry into London on Saturday, January 14th 1559. The Londoners welcomed her with pageants celebrating her as their Deborah, 'the judge and restorer of the house of Israel'. At one point the English Bible was presented to her. The coronation took place on the next day and was performed by the Bishop of Carlisle, the only one of Mary's bishops who would carry out the ceremony.*

**14**

The Queen's entry into London

Verse from William Birch, 'A Song between the Queen's Majesty and England, 1559'

**15**

The Queen presides at her coronation banquet in Westminster Hall

**16**

THE QUEEN SITS FOR HER PORTRAIT

Miniature by Nicholas Hilliard, 1572

*Nicholas Hilliard was the Queen's miniaturist. This is his earliest portrait of her and probably the occasion when she forcefully expressed her views on painting. Hilliard*

*writes that she 'chose her place to sit in for that purpose the open alley of a goodly garden where no tree was near, nor any shadow at all'.*

## 17

### ELIZABETH AND THE PHOENIX
Painting attributed to Nicholas Hilliard, c. 1575

*From her carcanet hangs a pendant jewel depicting a phoenix. This exotic and unique bird renewed itself by arising reborn from the ashes of its own funeral pyre. The Queen adopted the phoenix as an emblem of herself, as unique as she was chaste.*

## 18

### THE QUEEN HUNTS
The French ambassador describes the Queen hunting at Woodstock, 1575
The Earl of Leicester to Lord Burghley, 1575
The Queen receives news from a huntsman
The Queen at the kill

*'Her Majesty is very well,' wrote an observer in September 1600, 'and exceedingly disposed to hunting, for every second or third day she is on horseback, and continues the sport long.' Even at sixty-eight she rode ten miles a day on horseback and hunted.*

## 19

### THE QUEEN'S GARDENS
Lupold von Wedel describes the garden at Whitehall Palace, 1584
Thomas Platter describes the gardens at Nonsuch Palace, 1599

Views of the Great Garden at Whitehall
The Diana Fountain at Nonsuch Palace

*Each of the royal palaces had both public and privy gardens. The privy garden was the Queen's private garden and in this she would take the air or even conduct an interview with an ambassador. Each palace had a large park attached to it and Elizabeth remained a vigorous walker until the end of her life. In 1601 Rowland Whyte writes, 'The queen at Greenwich uses to walk much in the park, and takes great walks out of the park, and round the park.'*

## 20

### THE QUEEN'S FLOWERS
*Flowers fill the portraits of Elizabeth I, whether tucked in her hair, pinned to her dress or in the form of embroidery. As a Tudor she was always associated with the rose but as the reign progressed spring flowers were used more and more to celebrate the perpetual springtime of peace that she had brought to her kingdom. Courtiers presented flower jewels to her at New Year's Tide and poets sang of her as 'Beautie's rose' or 'Flora, Empresse of flowers'.*

## 21

### THE QUEEN AND THE PELICAN
Painting attributed to Nicholas Hilliard, c. 1575

*At her breast the Queen wears a jewel in the form of a pelican, a bird which in legend was supposed to feed its young by tearing at its breast rather than let them starve. Elizabeth used the pelican to symbolise her care for her people.*

## THE QUEEN'S PALACES

View of Nonsuch with Elizabeth in her coach

View of Greenwich from the river

### 23

Elizabeth walks in the procession of the Knights of the Garter with Windsor Castle in the distance

View of Whitehall from the river

*Elizabeth had five main palaces, Greenwich, Hampton Court, Whitehall, Windsor and Nonsuch. These she inherited. She never herself spent money on building but descriptions of the interiors suggest that she had strong views on their decoration which was lavish in its use of fabrics and gilding. Magnificence lay in the profuse array of tapestries, hangings, cushions and upholstery thickly embroidered with gold and silver.*

### 24

## THE QUEEN'S JEWELS

Painting attributed to William Segar, 1585

*Carcanet, black pearls and pendant from the Ermine Portrait. The black pearls, ones whose tinge was 'like that of black muscat grapes', had belonged to Mary Queen of Scots. Elizabeth purchased them from Mary's half-brother, the Earl of Moray. From her carcanet hangs one of the most legendary of all Tudor royal jewels, the Three Brothers, named after the three huge rubies. The Brethren had belonged to the Dukes of Burgundy and was later sold to Henry VIII. Elizabeth's successor, James I, wore it in his hat.*

### 25

## THE QUEEN LOSES HER JEWELS

Wardrobe Book of Elizabeth I

### 26 and 27

## NEW YEAR'S GIFTS TO THE QUEEN, 1589

*A selection of the gifts presented to Elizabeth on January 1st. Even the humblest officers of the household could give the Queen a gift. In return they received money or plate.*

### 28

## THE QUEEN'S MUSIC

Sir James Melville describes Elizabeth playing the virginals, 1564

Elizabeth playing the lute, by Nicholas Hilliard, c. 1580

*Elizabeth was a reasonably accomplished musician. She played both virginals and lute, could sing and compose. The Chapels Royal were the mainstay of music and musicians in Elizabethan England and nearly all the great composers of the period were members. Elizabeth herself was responsible for the maintenance and encouragment of church music. Much was composed in her honour, notably the madrigal series entitled* The Triumphs of Oriana *(1601).*

### 29

## THE QUEEN DANCES

Monsieur de Maisse talks to the Queen about dancing, 1597

*Elizabeth danced all her life. A month before she died she was still able to foot a coranto and*

she always delighted in watching good dancing. In September 1602 such gaiety continued unabated: 'We are here frolic at court, much dancing in the privy chamber, of country dances, before the Queen's majesty, who is exceedingly pleased therewith.'

## 30 and 31

### THE QUEEN'S FANS

Some of the fans listed in the Queen's wardrobe list of 1600

## 32

### FEET AND PETTICOATS

## 33

### AN EMBROIDERED BODICE

Detail from the Rainbow Portrait attributed to Marcus Gheeraerts, c. 1600

*Elizabeth, like other ladies, practised the art of embroidery. She sent Henry IV of France a scarf embroidered by herself.*

## 34 and 35

### THE QUEEN'S WARDROBE

Some items from the list of her clothes compiled in 1600

## 36 and 37

### THE QUEEN TRAVELS

Queen Elizabeth I carried in a litter, attributed to Robert Peake, c. 1600

*Elizabeth travelled a great deal, on horseback and by litter. A German saw her enter London in 1584 in a golden coach open on all sides with a canopy embroidered with gold and pearls. Later he saw her open Parliament in a wooden litter with cloth of gold and silver cushions.*

## 38 and 39

### THE FACE AND HANDS OF THE QUEEN

Monsieur de Maisse discusses the Queen, 1597

*Although there are numerous paintings of the Queen, descriptions of her by contemporaries are few. These begin in 1557 with a Venetian describing her at the age of twenty-three as 'comely rather than handsome, but she is tall and well-formed, with a good skin, although swarthy, she has fine eyes'. Over forty years later another Italian ungallantly refers to her as 'short, and ruddy in complexion; very strongly built'. Finally de Maisse draws a vivid picture of her at sixty-four: 'As for her face, it is and appears to be very aged. It is long and thin, and her teeth are very yellow and unequal . . . Her figure is fair and tall and graceful in whatever she does.'*

## 40 and 41

### THREE ROYAL FACES

Miniature by Nicholas Hilliard, c. 1600 (above)

Miniature by Isaac Oliver, c. 1590 (below)

Detail from the Ditchley Portrait by Marcus Gheeraerts the Younger, c. 1592

*As the Queen grew older painters were faced with the problem of reconciling the idea of the Queen with the reality. Her concern over her own image is reflected in the Privy Council's order in 1596 to destroy all portraits of her which were to her 'great offence'.*

## 42

### PAUL HENTZNER DESCRIBES THE QUEEN, 1598

Design by Nicholas Hilliard for a Great Seal of Ireland, c. 1595

*Hentzner's description records the Queen going in procession to chapel at Greenwich one Sunday morning.*

## 43

### THE QUEEN'S CHARACTER

Description by Sir John Hayward

Woodcut portrait surrounded by branches of eglantine, 1588

## 44

### A ROYAL JEWEL

Miniature by Nicholas Hilliard mounted within a case of enamelled gold set with diamonds and rubies

*By tradition this was given to Sir Thomas Heneage by the Queen on the defeat of the Spanish Armada in 1588. Jewels such as this, containing an idealised portrait of their sovereign, were frequently carried by courtiers.*

## 45

### THE QUEEN VISITS DITCHLEY, 1592

Painting by Marcus Gheeraerts, c. 1592

*This portrait was traditionally painted to commemorate the Queen's visit to Sir Henry Lee, her Master of the Armoury, at Ditchley in Oxfordshire in 1592. Her feet rest on that county in the picture. The visit was the occasion for a famous entertainment in which the Queen dispelled enchantments and thus awoke her host from a magical slumber. She symbolically banishes storms behind her and ushers in golden sunshine.*

## 46 and 47

### THE QUEEN GIVES AUDIENCE

Monsieur de Maisse describes being received by the Queen, 1597

The Queen informally receives two Dutch ambassadors, c. 1565

*Much of the Queen's day was consumed in granting audience, either formally in the Presence Chamber or informally in the Privy Chamber.*

## 48

### THE QUEEN IN MIDDLE AGE

Painting attributed to John Bettes, c. 1585–1590

## 49

### GODFREY GOODMAN SEES THE QUEEN, 1588

Goodman, then a young man studying law, saw the Queen leaving Somerset House one December evening in the year of the Armada

## 50

### ELIZA TRIUMPHANS, 1596

Engraving by Crispin van de Passe

## 51

### THE QUEEN ADDRESSES HER TROOPS, 1588

Speech by the Queen at Tilbury, 1588

*On August 9th Elizabeth reviewed her troops at Tilbury on horseback, wearing a steel breast-plate, and with a page bearing a helmet with white plumes walking behind her. She inspected the ranks of her soldiers 'like a woman, and anon with the countenance and pace of a soldier'. 'Her presence and her words,' William Camden records, 'fortified the courage of the captains and soldiers beyond all belief.'*

## 52

### A POEM BY THE QUEEN

One of the two poems known to have been written by Elizabeth, the other being composed 'upon Monsieur's departure'

## 53

A glass plaque with a bouquet of the Queen's flowers

## 54

### JOHN CLAPHAM DESCRIBES THE QUEEN

Miniature by Nicholas Hilliard, *c.* 1600

John Clapham was in the service of the Queen's first minister, Lord Burghley, and gives the most perceptive account of her character

## 55

### ROSA ELECTA

Engraving by William Rogers, *c.* 1595–1600

*The Queen was perpetually celebrated as the rose but she took for her personal use the eglantine, a single white rose, emblematic of her virginity. On the anniversary of her accession in 1590 a pillar was erected in the tiltyard, embraced by an eglantine tree.*

## 56 and 57

### THE QUEEN'S PROGRESSES

Sir Robert Sidney writes to Sir John Harington describing the Queen's visit to his house, 1600

*Throughout her reign Elizabeth indulged in spectacular summer progresses, in her early years visiting Oxford and Cambridge, Bristol and Norwich, so that her people might see her. Nobles and gentry vied with each other in providing yet more splendid entertainments. The most magnificent of these was Leicester's reception of her at Kenilworth in 1575. After the Armada these summer journeys were nearly all to private houses. Many were the occasions for elegant alfresco fêtes in which the Queen was celebrated as some visiting deity. She also had an appetite for private visits of the sort young Robert Sidney describes.*

## 58 and 59

### THE QUEEN'S ATTRIBUTES

*Elizabeth had a passion for allegory and symbol, a preoccupation shared by her poets who made her the subject of a cult. All this was summed up by Edmund Spenser in his epic poem* The Faerie Queene *in which he defines the dual nature of Elizabeth as 'a most royall queene or empresse' and as 'a most vertuous and bewtifull ladie'.*

The sieve is the attribute of the vestal virgin Tuccia. She had proved her chastity by carrying water from the river Tiber to the Vestal Temple in a sieve without spilling one drop. Elizabeth appears in several of her portraits carrying a sieve.

The globe is an emblem of the Queen's expanding empire, by the end of the reign stretching into the New World.

The ermine is a symbol of virginity. Rather than spoil its white fur it would die.

The rainbow is the emblem of peace. It promises calm after storms.

The serpent is the emblem of wisdom and prudence.

## 60

### SAINT ELIZABETH

Engraving by Francis Delaram, c. 1617–19

After her death she was hailed as a saint and acclaimed as 'In earth the first, in heaven the second maid.'

## 61

### THE QUEEN AND HER GODCHILD, 1576

'Boy Jack' or John Harington was one of the Queen's godchildren. His parents, John and Isabella Harington, had been imprisoned in the Tower in Mary's reign with the Princess Elizabeth. She sends him a copy of her speech to Parliament in which she declined their request for her to marry. Harington was fifteen at the time.

## 62

### THE QUEEN ADDRESSES PARLIAMENT, 1601

The celebrated Golden Speech, the last time Elizabeth addressed Parliament. At the opening on October 27th 1601 her enfeebled body had been unable to support the weight of her robes and she had been prevented from sinking to the ground by a nearby peer. The session was a stormy one with a vigorous attack on monopolies. On November 30th a deputation of a hundred and forty from the Commons waited on her at Whitehall to tender thanks for her promise to remedy this evil. In reply the Queen made one of the most moving speeches of her life.

## 63

### THE QUEEN IN OLD AGE

Detail from a posthumous painting by an unknown artist, c. 1610

## 64

### THE QUEEN'S DEATH

John Manningham refers to the Queen's death in his diary

Gloves presented to the Queen by the University of Oxford

Elizabeth died on March 24th 1603 at Richmond Palace. In January she had caught a bad cold and, following the warning of her astrologer John Dee to avoid Whitehall, she had moved to Richmond on a wet stormy day. On February 28th she began to sicken again and fever, sleeplessness, thirst and an immovable melancholy set in. For four days she remained on cushions on the floor refusing to be moved and in a state of semi-trance until, weak and emaciated, she was carried to her bed. After indicating the King of Scots as her successor, Archbishop Whitgift prayed at her bedside until she sank into a deep slumber. At about three in the morning of March 24th it was found that she was dead.

# Image Index

All are portraits of Elizabeth I unless stated. For further details the reader is referred to Roy Strong's *Portraits of Queen Elizabeth I* (Oxford, 1963).

The Royal Collection, reproduced by gracious permission of Her Majesty The Queen: Circle of William Scrots, Windsor Castle (9, 26, 38), Family of Henry VIII by an unknown artist (11, 19, 56), by the Monogrammist HE (26).

Arbury Hall, by permission of Mr F. H. M. FitzRoy-Newdegate (25, 30, 48); Ashmolean Museum, Oxford: views by Wyngaerde (21, 22, 23), the Queen's gloves (64); Berkeley Castle, by kind permission of the Trustees of The 8th Earl of Berkeley deceased (28); British Museum, by courtesy of the Trustees of the British Museum: View of Nonsuch by Hoefnagel (22), Garter Procession by Marcus Gheeraerts (23), Great Seal by Hilliard (42), Coronation Procession, Egerton MS 3320 (14, 15); Cambridge, Trinity College, by permission of the Master and Fellows (27, 30, 32); College of Arms, by permission of the Chapter: MS M.6 (14, 15, 18); Corsham Court, by permission of Lord Methuen (63); Greenwich, National Maritime Museum (12, 25); Hardwick Hall, by permission of the National Trust (26, 27, 30, 32, 34, 35, 39, 56, 57); Hatfield House, by courtesy of The Marquess of Salisbury, KG: attributed to Segar (24, 39, 59), attributed to Marcus Gheeraerts (26, 33, 39, 59); Helmingham Hall, by permission of Lord Tollemache (30); Kassel, Staatliche Kunstsammlungen (46–7, 56, 57); Liverpool, Walker Art Gallery (25, 58); Loseley House, by permission of Mr J. R. More Molyneux (53); National Portrait Gallery: No 108 (16, 20, 38), No 190 (17, 27), No 200 (20), No 2082 (12, 38, 39), No 2471 (30, 39), No 2561 (20, 25, 26, 32, 41, 45); The Earl of Scarbrough: The Red Book (19); Siena, Pinacoteca Nazionale (25, 34, 58); Sherborne Castle, by permission of Mr Simon Wingfield Digby (26, 36–7); Tatton Park, by permission of the National Trust (38); Victoria & Albert Museum, Crown Copyright: by Hilliard (40), by Oliver (40), Armada Jewel (44); Warwick Castle, by permission of Lord Brooke (13); Welbeck Abbey, by permission of The Duke of Portland (30, 32, 56, 57); Woburn Abbey, by permission of The Duke of Bedford (12, 56, 57, 58); Yale, the Elizabethan Club, by permission of the Board of Governors (26, 27, 30, 34).

All borders and decorations are from contemporary books.